Fireboat

The Heroic Adventures of the John J. Harvey

by Maira Kalman

G. P. Putnam's Sons
An Imprint of Penguin Group (USA) Inc.

New York City.
1931.

Amazing things
were happening
big and <small>small.</small>

The Empire State Building　　　went up

up

up.

Babe Ruth hit his 611th home run in Yankee Stadium.

The tasty candy treat
Snickers
hit the
stores.

The George Washington Bridge was suspended

elegantly across the mighty Hudson River.

Champion Pendley Calling of Blarney

won Best in Show at the Westminster Kennel Club.

On a hot
and jazzy night
the word
HOT-CHA
was
invented.

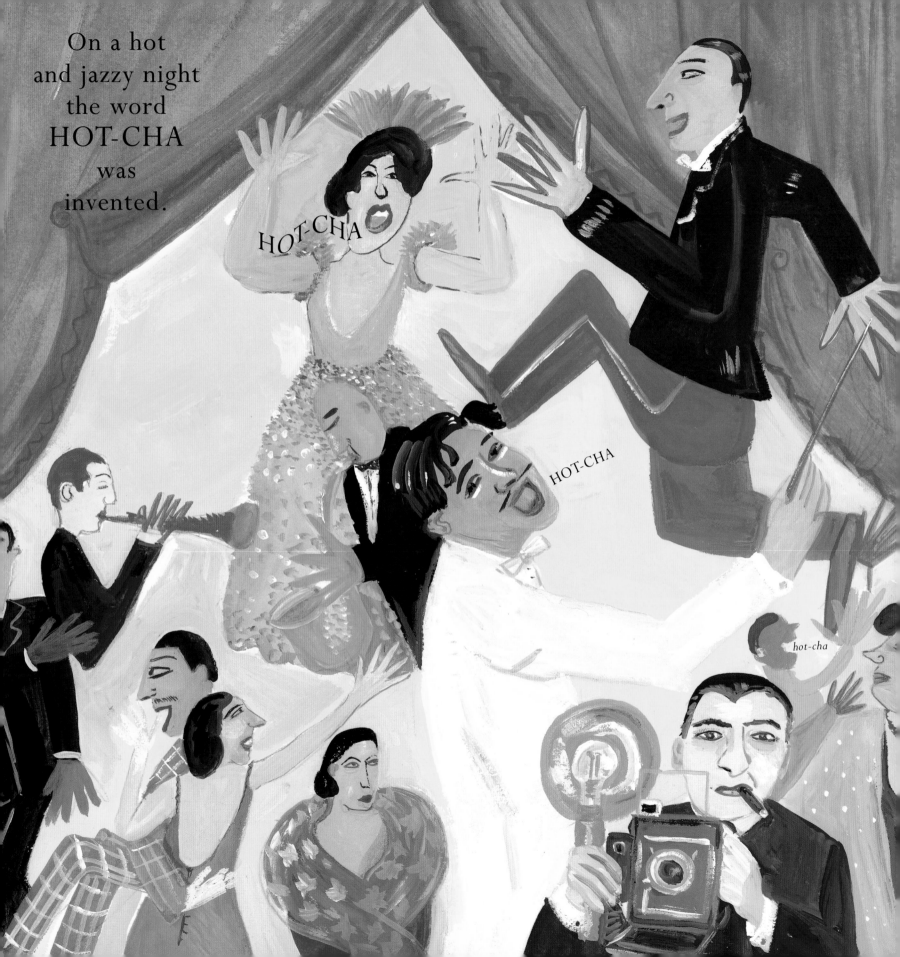

And on a sunny fresh day, the
John J. Harvey fireboat
was launched.

There were 12 fireboats in
New York City. The Harvey was
the largest, fastest and shiniest
fireboat of them all.

It had 5 diesel engines so it could go 20 miles per hour. (that's pretty fast!)

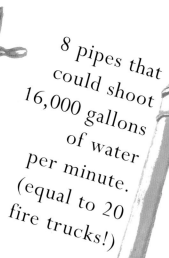

8 pipes that could shoot 16,000 gallons of water per minute. (equal to 20 fire trucks!)

A completely round steering wheel.

A control dial in the pilot's cabin.

Many brass nozzles housed in the gold room.

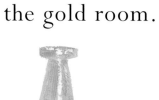

A very nice can to oil all squeaks,

ropes (called lines),

and lots of levers, buttons, and buckets.

There was a pilot and a crew ready in 2 minutes to fight the fires.

They were a brave group.

And there was a dog named Smokey, who did not put out the fires but had many nice spots.

The Harvey went up and down the river, fighting fires.
It fought fires at the bustling piers.

The piers were the places where
ships and trains brought all manner of
merchandise to be sold in the city. Like wood and
cotton and bananas and bubble gum and
EVERYTHING.

It fought the fire of the great ocean
liner NORMANDIE.

Sometimes the Harvey just went out to shoot water in **celebration**.

Many years passed. A new captain had come on board, Bob Lenney. He and his crew fought many fires. But New York was changing. The Twin Towers were now the tallest buildings in New York City. The piers were closing.

1995.
The city no longer needed so many fireboats.
The Harvey was considered old and useless.
It sat in the water for five years
waiting to be sold for scrap.

And then a very surprising thing
happened. A group of friends
were eating at a restaurant
called Florent.

They had heard about the
fireboat and decided something.
"Let's save the Harvey. Let's buy her!
Everyone needs a fireboat. We won't
put out fires, we'll just have fun."
And they did!

They took it to Caddell's ship
repair yard in Staten Island.
Even there they said, "She is
old. It will be hard to fix her."
But the owners said, "Fix!"
So they fixed! Beautifully.

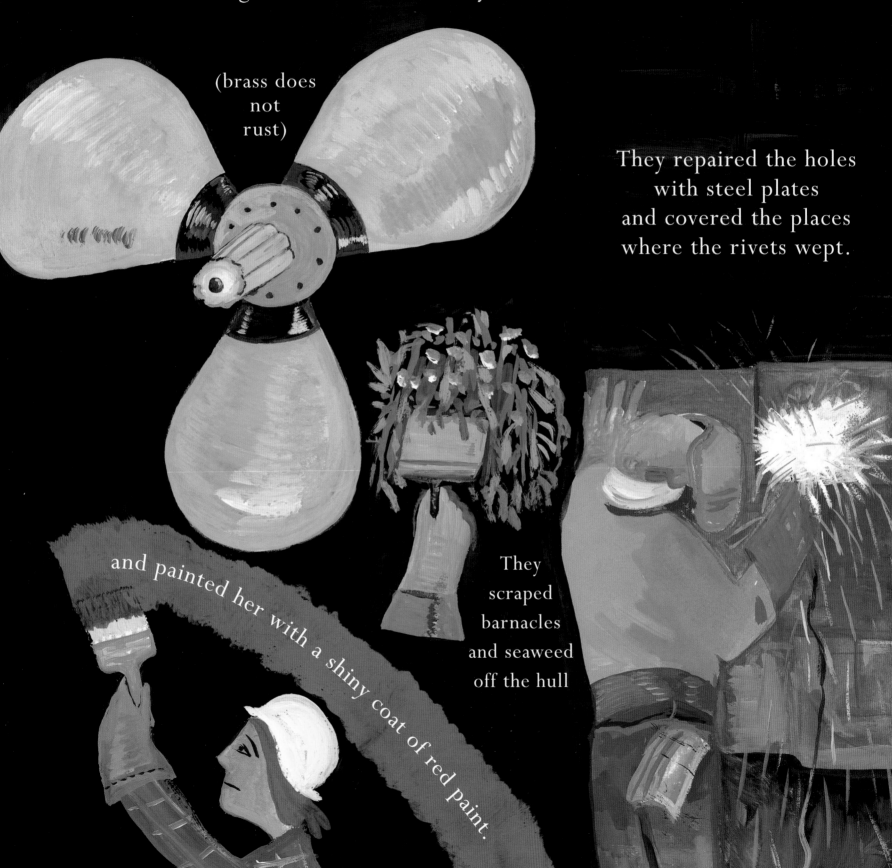

They repaired the 2 propellers
making them new with a shiny coat of brass.

(brass does
not
rust)

They repaired the holes
with steel plates
and covered the places
where the rivets wept.

and painted her with a shiny coat of red paint.

They
scraped
barnacles
and seaweed
off the hull

And once again the Harvey
was on the water.

Tim the engineer keeping
things running smoothly.

Jessica the assistant engineer
at the controls in the
noisy engine room.

Andrew welding.

Chase helping.

John fixing.

Tom cooking.

Huntley at
the wheel.

And Bob Lenney
watching over
everyone and
being very proud.

They made friends with
the only other fireboats on
the river, the Fire Fighter
and the McKean.

Everyone said, "The
Harvey is a nice old
boat, but she could
NEVER be used to
fight a fire.
NEVER."

toot toot toot toot toot

(A boat says hello
with four toots)

But then on September 11, 2001
something so huge and horrible
happened that the whole world
shook.

It was 8:45 in the morning,
another beautiful and sunny day.

Two airplanes
    crashed into the Twin Towers.
        CRASHED, CRASHED, CRASHED into these two strong buildings.

The sky filled with fire and smoke.
The buildings exploded and
fell down to the ground.
Many people were hurt.

Many lives were lost.

The news spread. The city had been attacked. Everyone was terrified.
But people were brave. The entire city sprang into action.

Firefighters and police officers and doctors

and construction workers

and teachers

and children

and cooks

and parents.

The mayor was strong. He said, "We will all work together. We will not be broken."

What were the people of the Harvey doing when the planes hit?

Bob Lenney was trimming hedges.

Tom was drinking tea in his kitchen.

Chase was walking his dog Radar.

Tim was reading the paper.

Andrew was welding.

Jessica was writing a story.

John was working.

Huntley was reading *David Copperfield*.

The Harvey was snoozing at the pier.

They all had one thought. Get to the Harvey. And they did. They called the fire department. "John J. Harvey, ready to help. How can we help?" The answer came: "You can't help fight the fire but you can ferry people to safety."

But suddenly an urgent message
came loud and clear. "John J. Harvey.
Where are you? We need you,
WE NEED YOU!"

The water pipes were broken and buried.
And the fire trucks that had raced to the
scene could not pump water. The
firefighters attached hoses to the Harvey.

The Harvey fought the fires
alongside the McKean
and the Fire Fighter.

For four days and nights the Harvey pumped water.
The crew took turns sleeping. People brought
supplies: fuel, sweaters, gloves, pizza,
sandwiches and coffee. They worked
and cried. They fought the fire
until it was under control.

Finally, it was time for
the Harvey to go home.

Everyone on the boat
had never seen anything
so terrible.

And they had never
felt so proud.

The Harvey was a hero.   And everyone knew it.

The Harvey won
an important award.

NATIONAL PRESERVATION AWARD

JOHN J. HARVEY

FOR CAPPING A DISTINGUISHED CAREER OF SERVICE
BY COMING OUT OF RETIREMENT TO PROVIDE
INVALUABLE AID IN NEW YORK CITY'S HOUR OF NEED.

October 18, 2001

At the ceremony the
audience cheered,
and some even cried.

Now the Twin Towers are gone.
Something new will be built.
The heroes who died will be remembered forever.
The Harvey is back to being a very happy boat.

NOT scrapped.

NOT useless.

NOT forgotten.

A proud and plucky
friend. And all
that's left to say is

HOT-CHA

(and thank you!)

Wait a minute.
There is something more to say.
The friends of the Harvey have found a
little tugboat to adopt.
Doesn't everyone need a tugboat?

G. P. PUTNAM'S SONS • A division of Penguin Young Readers Group.

Published by The Penguin Group. Penguin Group (USA) Inc., 375 Hudson Street, New York, NY 10014, U.S.A. Penguin Group (Canada), 90 Eglinton Avenue East, Suite 700, Toronto, Ontario M4P 2Y3, Canada (a division of Pearson Penguin Canada Inc.). Penguin Books Ltd, 80 Strand, London WC2R 0RL, England. Penguin Ireland, 25 St. Stephen's Green, Dublin 2, Ireland (a division of Penguin Books Ltd.). Penguin Group (Australia), 250 Camberwell Road Camberwell, Victoria 3124, Australia (a division of Pearson Australia Group Pty Ltd). Penguin Books India Pvt Ltd, 11 Community Centre, Panchsheel Park, New Delhi - 110 017, India. Penguin Group (NZ), 67 Apollo Drive, Rosedale, North Shore 0632, New Zealand (a division of Pearson New Zealand Ltd). Penguin Books (South Africa) (Pty) Ltd, 24 Sturdee Avenue, Rosebank, Johannesburg 2196, South Africa. Penguin Books Ltd, Registered Offices: 80 Strand, London WC2R 0RL, England.

Published simultaneously in Canada. Manufactured in China by South China Printing Co. Ltd.

Book designed by M&Co. Text set in Perpetua. The art was done in gouache.

Anniversary Edition, 2011.

Library of Congress Cataloging-in-Publication Data

Kalman, Maira. Fireboat: the heroic adventures of the John J. Harvey / Maira Kalman. p. cm. Summary: A fireboat, launched in 1931, is retired after many years of fighting fires along the Hudson River, but is saved from being scrapped and then called into service again on September 11, 2001. 1. John J. Harvey (Fireboat)—Juvenile literature. 2. September 11 Terrorist Attacks, 2001—Juvenile literature. 3. World Trade Center (New York, N.Y.) —Juvenile literature. [1. John J. Harvey (Fireboat) 2. Boats and boating. 3. Fire extinction. 4. September 11 Terrorist Attacks, 2001. 5. World Trade Center (New York, N.Y.)] I. Title. TH9391 .K35 2002 974.7 1044—dc21 2002002423

ISBN 978-0-399-23953-3

11 13 15 17 19 20 18 16 14 12 10

Thanks to the civic minded Florent Morellet for sharing this beautiful story with me.

Hats off to all the owners and volunteers of the Harvey—

David Beatty, Andrew Beatty,

John Doswell & Jean Preece, William Drawbridge, Rafe Evans,

Huntley Gill, Sergio Guardia, Tim Ivory, John & Angela Krevey,

Garry Pace, Marja Samsom,

Randy Simon, Eric & Bonnie Weisler, Chase Welles,

Robert Lenney, Andrew Furber, Tomas Cavallero,

Jessica DuLong, Pamela Hepburn,

Steven P. Kalil, FDNY Marine Companies One and Nine.

Thanks to Al Trojanowicz, Maritime Historian and retired member of the FDNY.

His assistance in researching this story was invaluable.

Kudos to Meaghan Kombol for research, design, production and general wisdom.

If you wish to contribute time or money or would like to visit the actual John J. Harvey,

go to the shipshape website www.Fireboat.org

for lulu and alex, my formidable shipmates.

FULL
HALF
STOP